# Hal Leonard EASY SONGS FOR MANDOLIN

## MANDOLIN METHOD
Supplement to Any Mandolin Method

Play the Melodies of 20 Pop, Bluegrass, Folk, Classical, and Blues Songs

BY RICH DELGROSSO

# INTRODUCTION

**W**elcome to *Easy Songs for Mandolin*, a collection of 20 pop, bluegrass, folk, classical, and blues favorites arranged for easy mandolin. If you're a beginning mandolin player, you've come to the right place; these well-known songs will have you playing, reading, and enjoying music in no time!

This collection can be used on its own or as a supplement to the *Hal Leonard Mandolin Method – 2nd Edition* or any other beginning mandolin method. The songs are arranged in order of difficulty. Each melody is presented in an easy-to-read format—including extra mandolin parts and guitar chord symbols for your teacher or friend to play along. As you progress through the book, you can go back and try playing these other parts as well.

ISBN 978-0-634-08738-7

HAL•LEONARD®
CORPORATION
7777 W. BLUEMOUND RD. P.O. BOX 13819 MILWAUKEE, WI 53213

Visit Hal Leonard Online at
**www.halleonard.com**

# SONG STRUCTURE

The songs in this book have different sections, which may or may not include the following:

## Intro
This is usually a short instrumental section that "introduces" the song at the beginning.

## Verse
This is one of the main sections of a song and conveys most of the storyline. A song usually has several verses, all with the same music but each with different lyrics.

## Chorus
This is often the most memorable section of a song. Unlike the verse, the chorus usually has the same lyrics every time it repeats.

## Bridge
This section is a break from the rest of the song, often having a very different chord progression and feel.

## Solo
This is an instrumental section, often played over the verse or chorus structure.

## Outro
Similar to an intro, this section brings the song to an end.

# ENDINGS & REPEATS

Many of the songs have some new symbols that you must understand before playing. Each of these represents a different type of ending.

## 1st and 2nd Endings
These are indicated by brackets and numbers. The first time through a song section, play the first ending and then repeat. The second time through, skip the first ending, and play through the second ending.

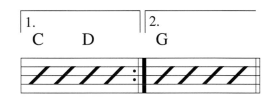

## D.S.
This means "Dal Segno" or "from the sign." When you see this abbreviation above the staff, find the sign ( 𝄋 ) earlier in the song and resume playing from that point.

## al Coda
This means "to the Coda," a concluding section in the song. If you see the words "D.S. al Coda," return to the sign ( 𝄋 ) earlier in the song and play until you see the words "To Coda," then skip to the Coda at the end of the song, indicated by the symbol: ⊕.

## al Fine
This means "to the end." If you see the words "D.S. al Fine," return to the sign ( 𝄋 ) earlier in the song and play until you see the word "Fine."

## D.C.
This means "Da Capo" or "from the head." When you see this abbreviation above the staff, return to the beginning (or "head") of the song and resume playing.

# CONTENTS

# PUFF THE MAGIC DRAGON

Words and Music by
LENNY LIPTON and PETER YARROW

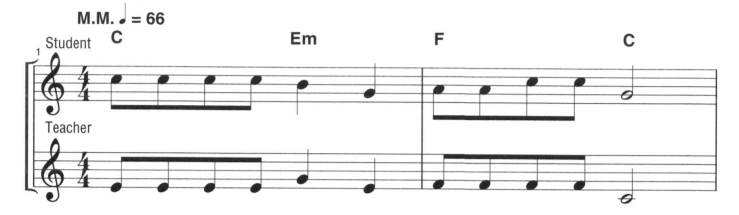

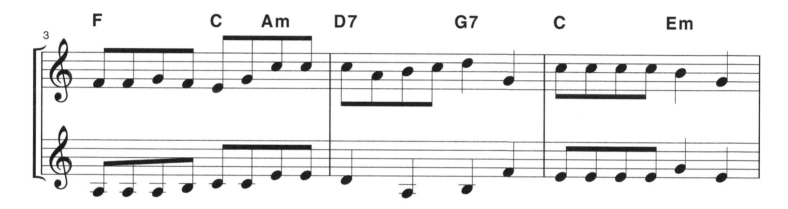

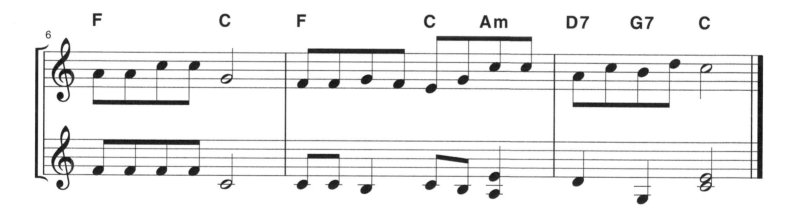

# LOVE ME TENDER

Words and Music by
ELVIS PRESLEY and VERA MATSON

**Verse**
M.M. ♩ = 110

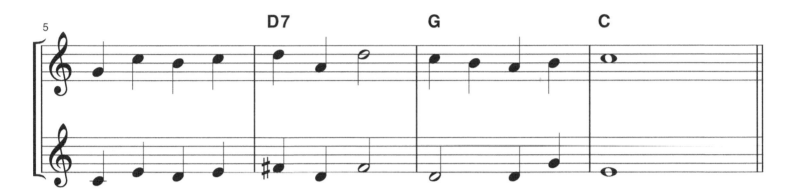

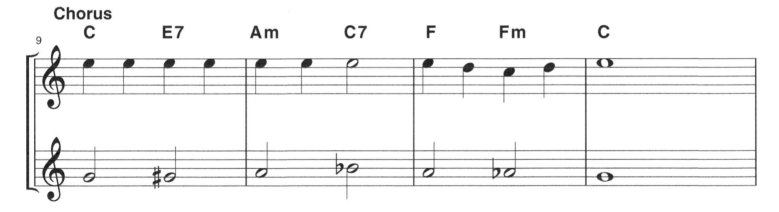

**Chorus**

# EVERY BREATH YOU TAKE

Music and Lyrics by
STING

M.M. ♩ = 118

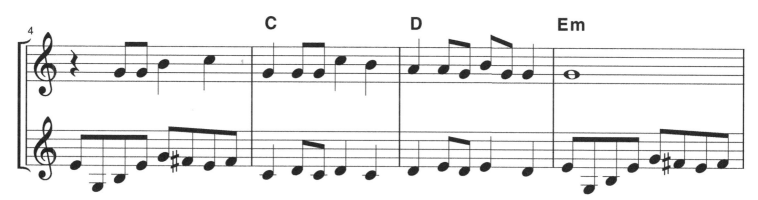

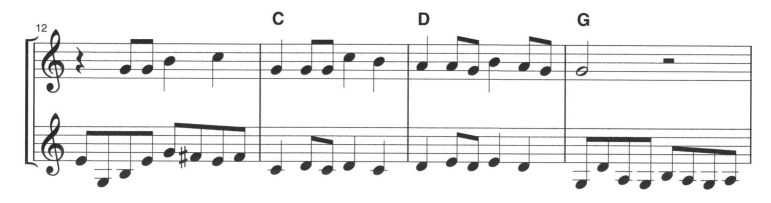

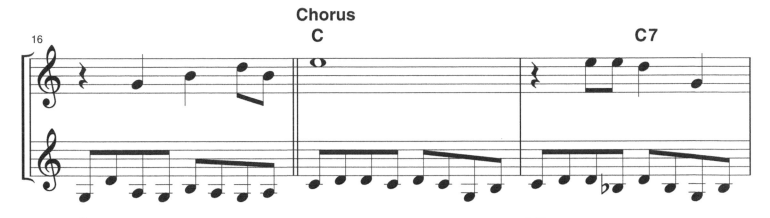

**Chorus**

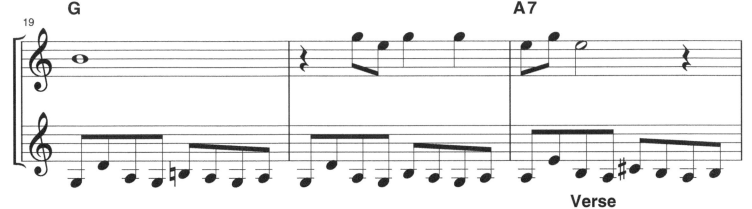

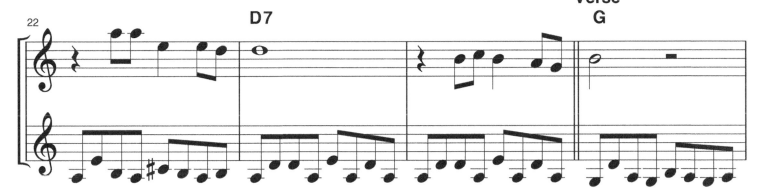

# WHERE HAVE ALL THE FLOWERS GONE?

Words and Music by
PETE SEEGER

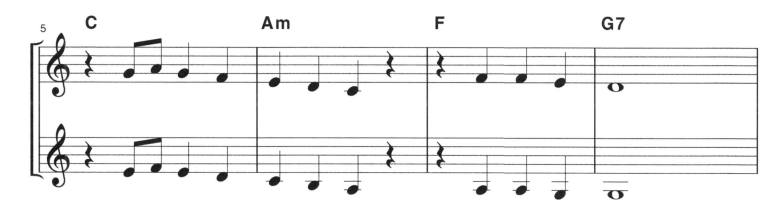

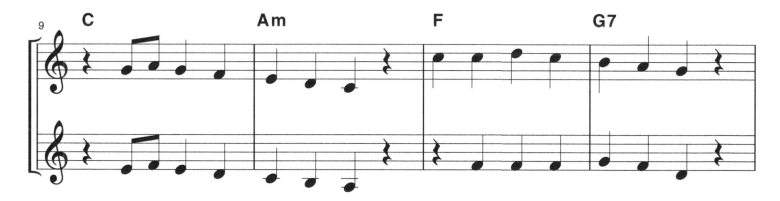

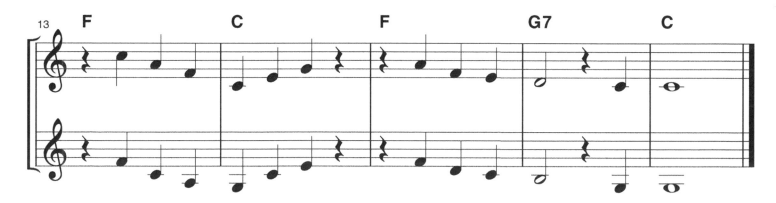

# MAGGIE MAY

Words and Music by
ROD STEWART and MARTIN QUITTENTON

M.M. ♩ = 120

Intro

Verse

Chorus

*Play 1st time only.

# ALL MY LOVING

Words and Music by
JOHN LENNON and PAUL McCARTNEY

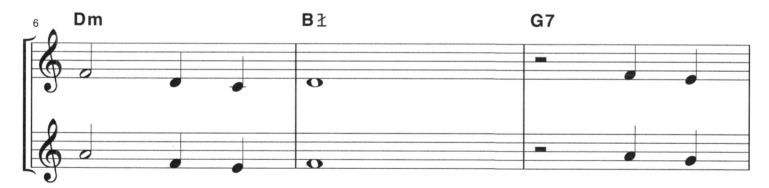

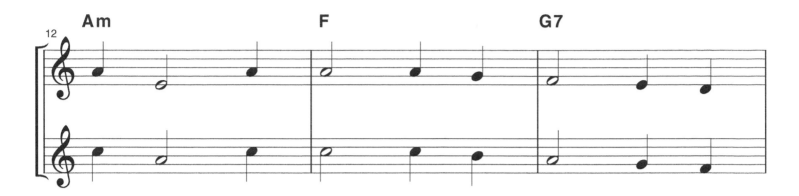

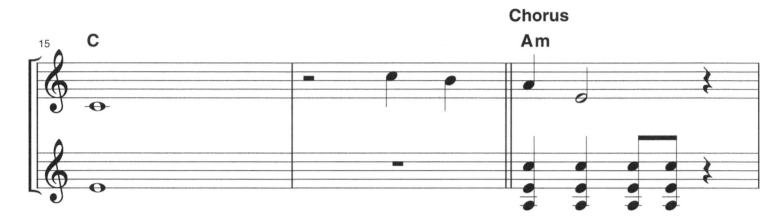

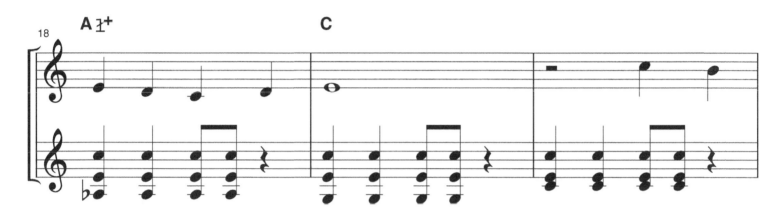

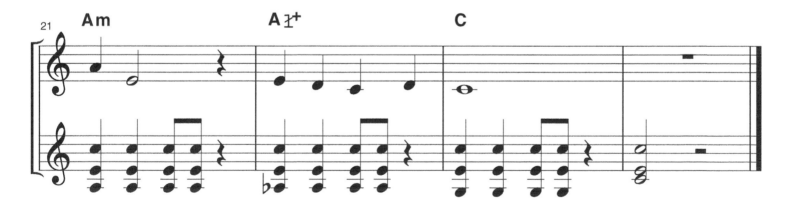

# LET IT BE
## (Duet)

Words and Music by
JOHN LENNON and PAUL McCARTNEY

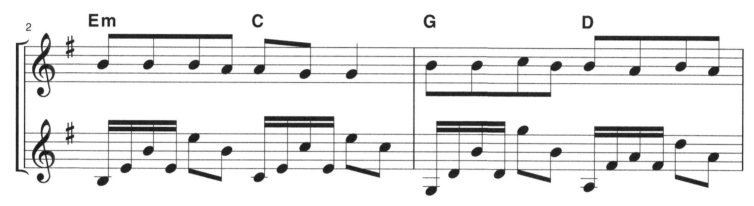

**Chorus**

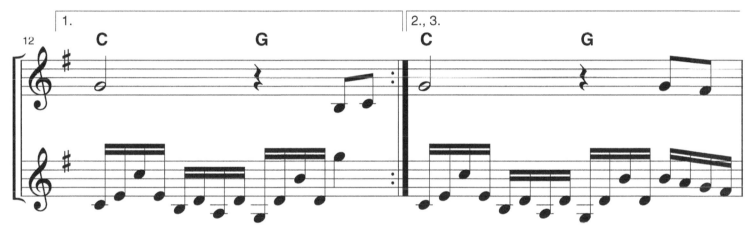

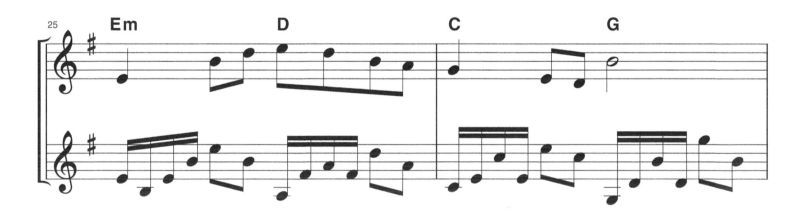

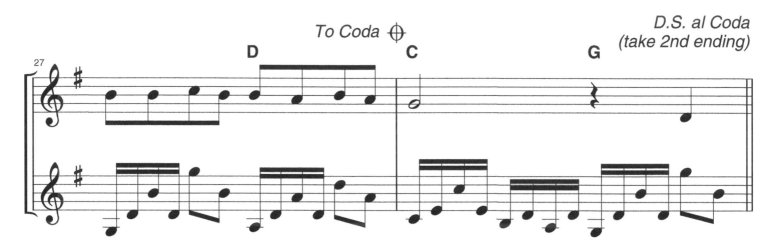

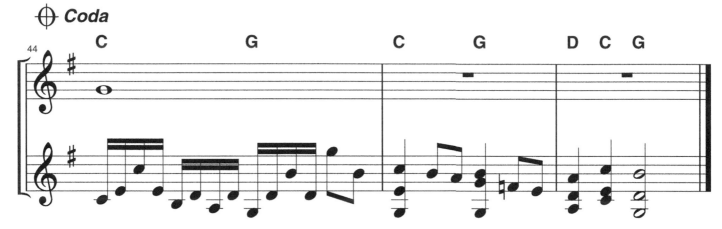

# THE HOUSE OF THE RISING SUN
## (Duet)

Words and Music by
ALAN PRICE

**Verse**

M.M. ♩ = 89

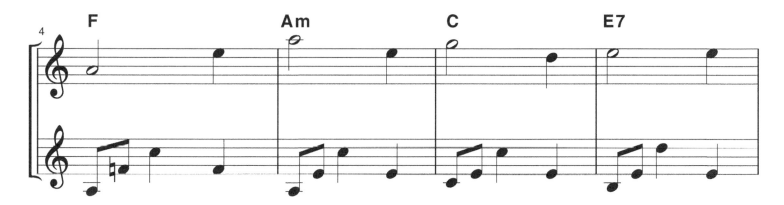

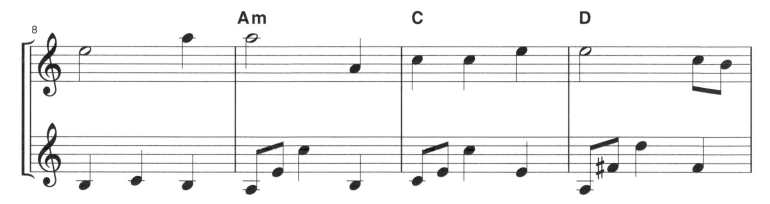

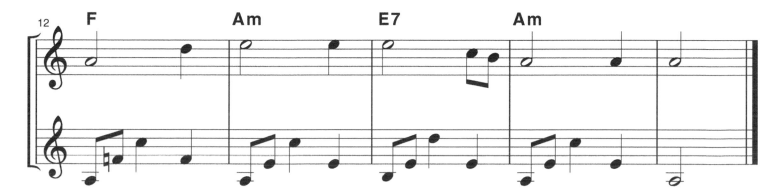

# NORWEGIAN WOOD
## (This Bird Has Flown)

Words and Music by
JOHN LENNON and PAUL McCARTNEY

**Verse**

M.M. ♩ =168

**Bridge**

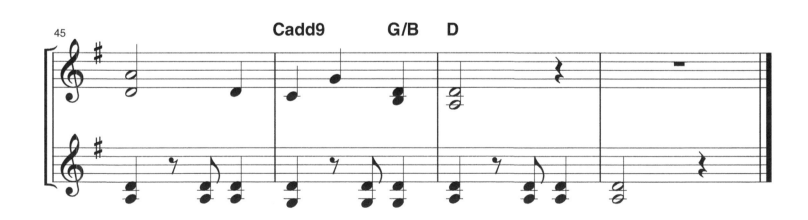

# SCARBOROUGH FAIR
## (Duet)

Traditional English

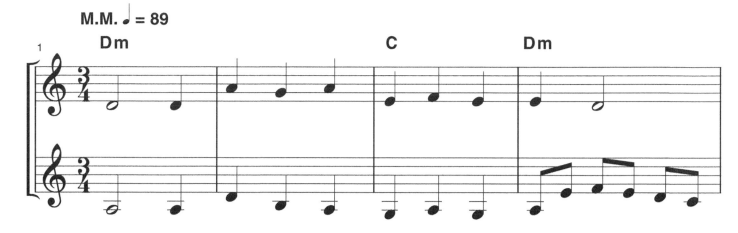

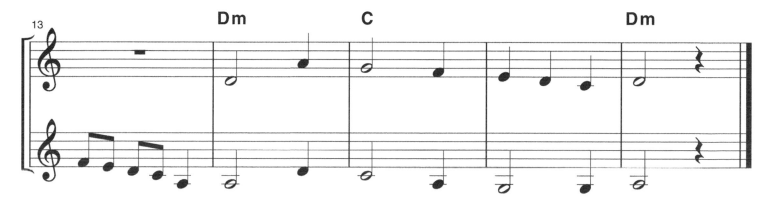

# SOUTHWIND
## (Celtic Air Solo)

Traditional

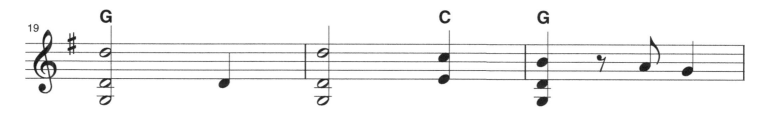

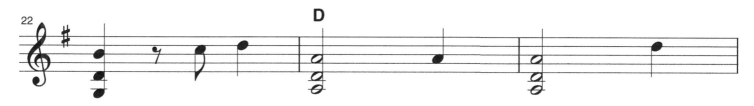

# BABY PLEASE DON'T GO
## (Blues Trio)

Words and Music by
JOSEPH LEE WILLIAMS

# SANTA LUCIA
## (Duet)

By TEODORO COTTRAU

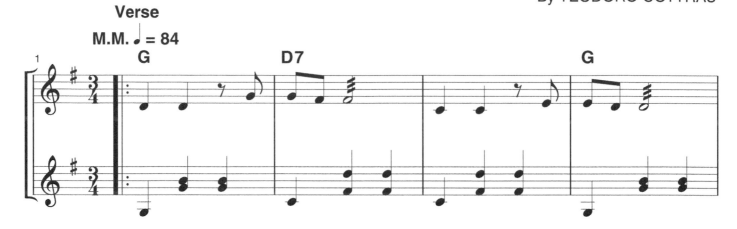

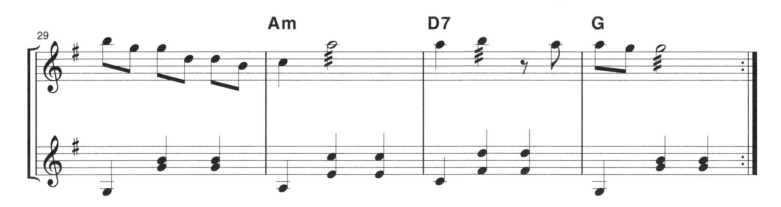

# TENNESSEE WALTZ
## (Duet)

Words and Music by
REDD STEWART and PEE WEE KING

**Swing feel**    **Verse**

M.M. ♩ = 83

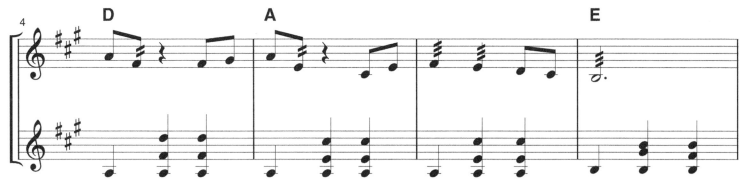

**Chorus**

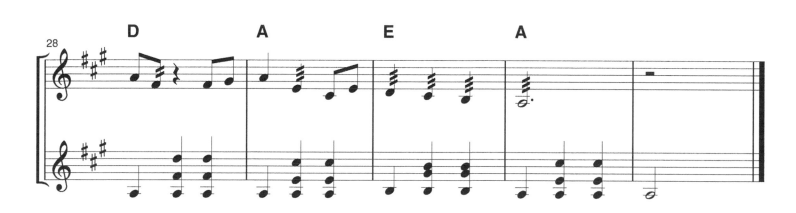

# CARELESS LOVE

Anonymous

**Swing feel**

M.M. ♩ = 118

**Verse**

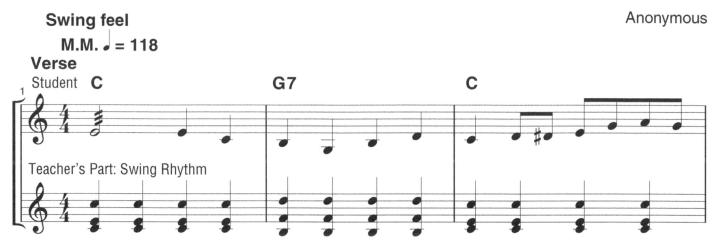

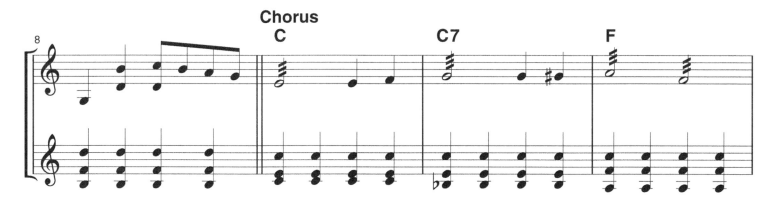

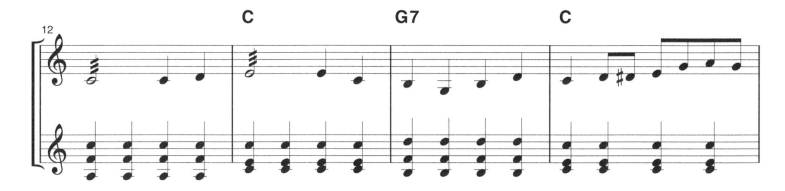

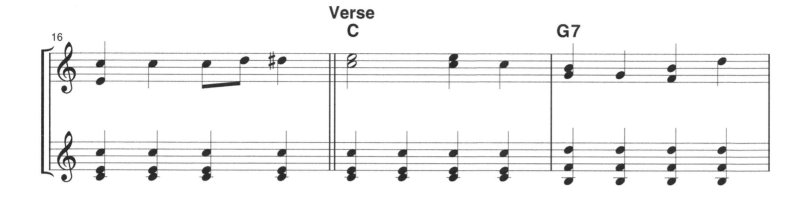

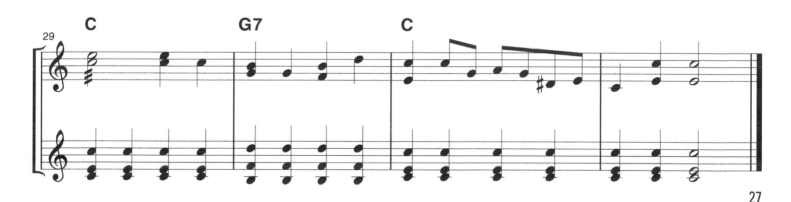

# ST. LOUIS BLUES

## (Duet)

Words and Music by
W. C. HANDY

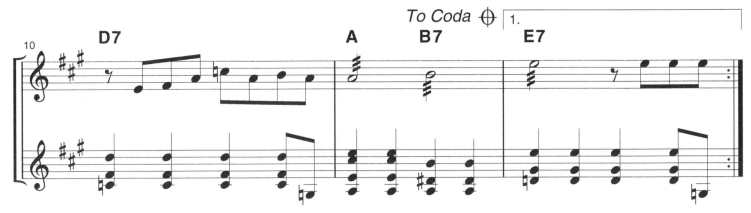

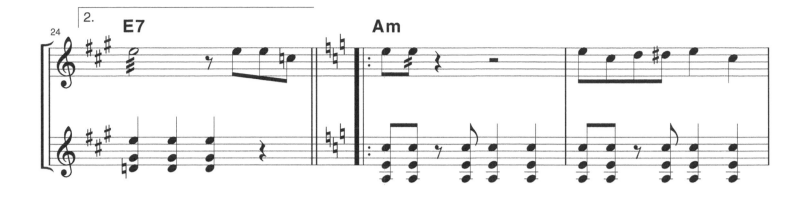

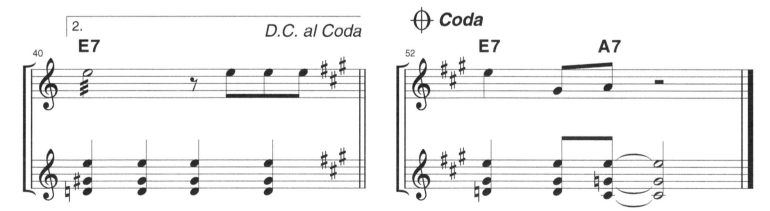

# ANNIE'S SONG
## (Duet)

Words and Music by<br>JOHN DENVER

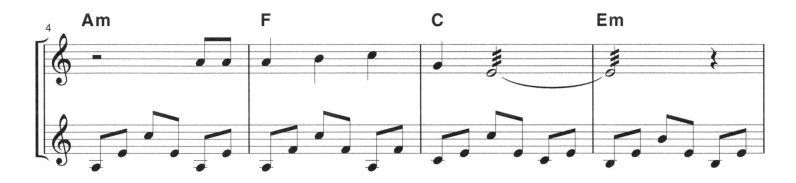

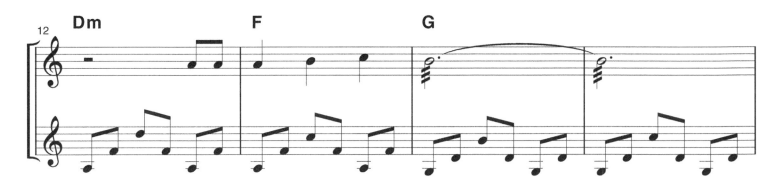

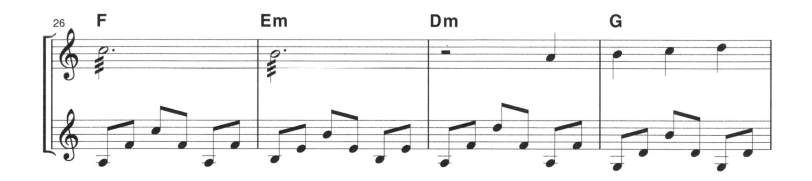

# CALIFORNIA DREAMIN'
## (Duet)

Words and Music by
JOHN PHILLIPS and MICHELLE PHILLIPS

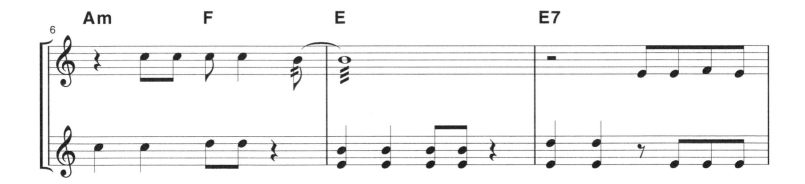

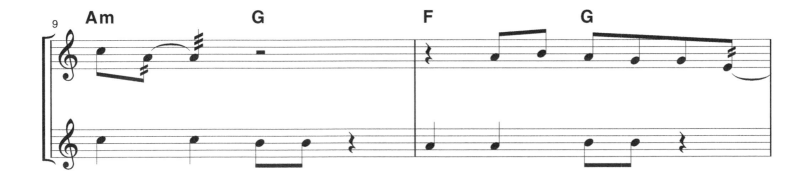

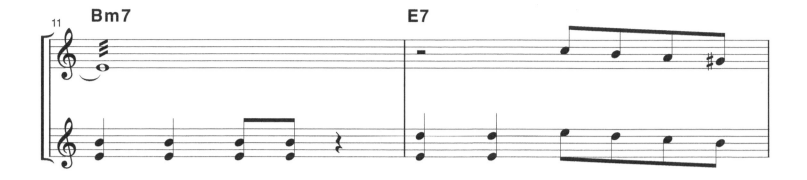

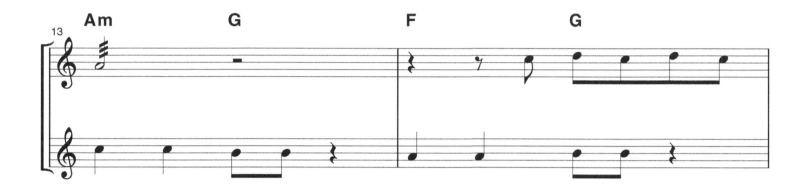

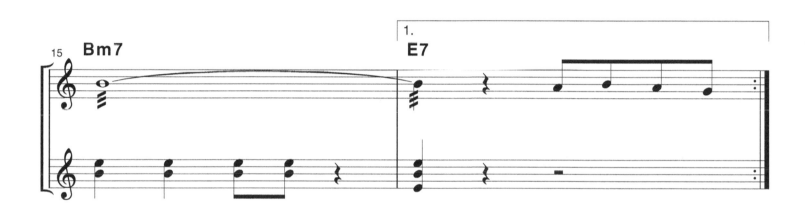

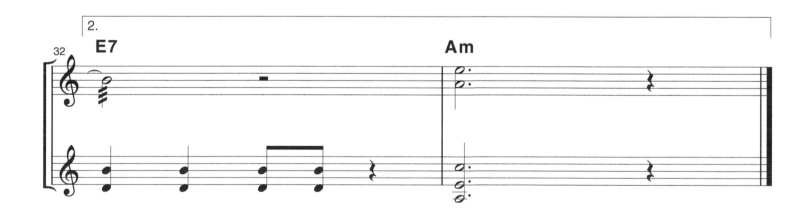

# MUSETTE
## (Duet)

By JOHANN SEBASTIAN BACH

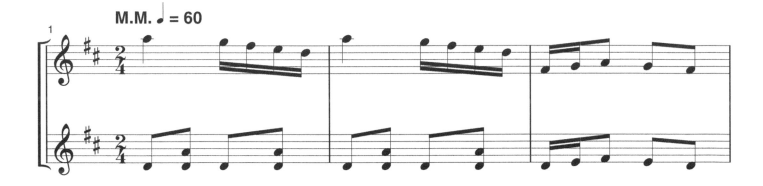

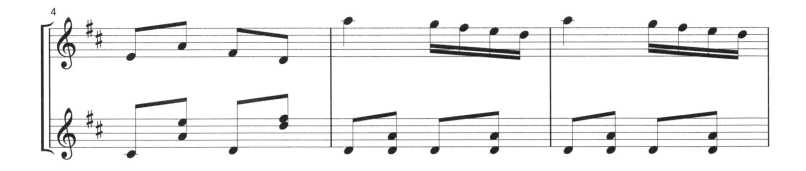

# KEEP ON THE SUNNY SIDE

Words and Music by
A. P. CARTER

M.M. ♩ = 84

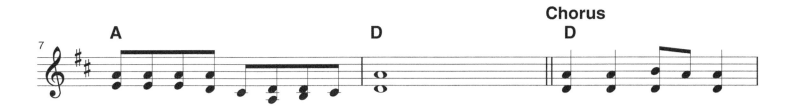

**Verse**

**Chorus**

# Great Mandolin Songbooks
## from Hal Leonard

### THE BEATLES FOR SOLO MANDOLIN

20 favorite Beatles tunes in chord melody arrangements for mandolin including: All You Need Is Love • Blackbird • Can't Buy Me Love • Eight Days a Week • Here Comes the Sun • Hey Jude • In My Life • Let It Be • Michelle • Strawberry Fields Forever • Twist and Shout • We Can Work It Out • Yesterday • and more.

00128672............................................... $16.99

### CHRISTMAS CAROLS FOR MANDOLIN

23 Christmas songs arranged especially for mandolin, including: Away in a Manger • The First Noel • God Rest Ye Merry, Gentlemen • Hark! the Herald Angels Sing • It Came upon the Midnight Clear • Jingle Bells • O Christmas Tree • O Holy Night • Silent Night • Up on the Housetop • We Wish You a Merry Christmas • What Child Is This? • and more.

00699800............................................... $10.99

### CLASSICAL SOLOS FOR MANDOLIN

This publication contains 20 classical mandolin pieces compiled, edited, and performed by world-renowned virtuoso Carlos Aonzo. The music is arranged in order of difficulty beginning with exercises by Giuseppe Branzoli and finishing with complete concert pieces using the most advanced mandolin techniques. Pieces include: Andante – Pizzicato on the Left Hand (Carlo Munier) • Exercise in A Major (Giuseppe Branzoli) • La Fustemberg (Antonio Riggeiri) • Partita V in G minor Overture (Filippo Sauli) • Theme with Variations in A Major (Bartolomeo Bortolazzi) • and more.

00124955  Book/Online Audio ......................... $19.99

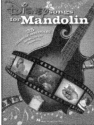

### DISNEY SONGS FOR MANDOLIN

25 classic melodies from Disney's finest productions over the years presented in arrangements for mandolin. Includes: The Bare Necessities • Be Our Guest • Circle of Life • Colors of the Wind • Go the Distance • Heigh-Ho • It's a Small World • Mickey Mouse March • A Spoonful of Sugar • Under the Sea • When You Wish upon a Star • Zip-A-Dee-Doo-Dah • and more.

00701904............................................... $12.99

### FIDDLE TUNES FOR FLATPICKERS: MANDOLIN

Now you can learn to play famous fiddle tunes specially arranged for mandolin. Get started flatpickin' now with songs like: Blackberry Blossom • Kentucky Mandolin • Old Joe Clark • Salt Creek • Turkey in the Straw • and more. The accompanying audio features specially mixed tracks that let you hear the mandolin alone, the mandolin with the backing track, or just the backing track so you can play along!

14011276  Book/Online Audio ........................ $17.99

### FIRST 50 SONGS YOU SHOULD PLAY ON MANDOLIN

A fantastic collection of 50 accessible, must-know favorites for the beginner who's learned enough to start playing popular songs: Amazing Grace • Crazy • Cripple Creek • Folsom Prison Blues • Friend of the Devil • Hallelujah • Ho Hey • I Am a Man of Constant Sorrow • I Walk the Line • I'll Fly Away • Losing My Religion • Maggie May • Mr. Bojangles • Rocky Top • Take Me Home, Country Roads • Tennessee Waltz • Wagon Wheel • Wildwood Flower • Yesterday • and more.

00155489  Tab, Chords & Lyrics ...................... $15.99

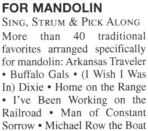

### FOLK SONGS FOR MANDOLIN

SING, STRUM & PICK ALONG

More than 40 traditional favorites arranged specifically for mandolin: Arkansas Traveler • Buffalo Gals • (I Wish I Was In) Dixie • Home on the Range • I've Been Working on the Railroad • Man of Constant Sorrow • Michael Row the Boat Ashore • My Old Kentucky Home • Oh! Susanna • She'll Be Comin' 'Round the Mountain • Turkey in the Straw • The Wabash Cannon Ball • When the Saints Go Marching In • Yankee Doodle • and more!

00701918............................................... $16.99

### THE HAL LEONARD MANDOLIN FAKE BOOK

This collection packs 300 songs into one handy songbook: As Time Goes By • Bad, Bad Leroy Brown • Can't Take My Eyes off of You • Daydream Believer • Edelweiss • Fields of Gold • Going to California • Hey, Soul Sister • Ho Hey • I'm Yours • Island in the Sun • King of the Road • Losing My Religion • Maggie May • Over the Rainbow • Peaceful Easy Feeling • Redemption Song • Shenandoah • Toes • Unchained Melody • Wildwood Flower • You Are My Sunshine • and many more.

00141053  Melody, Lyrics & Chords .............. $39.99

### MASTERS OF THE MANDOLIN

This collection of 130 mandolin solos is an invaluable resource for fans of bluegrass music. Each song excerpt has been meticulously transcribed note-for-note in tab from its original recording so you can study and learn these masterful solos by some of the instrument's finest pickers. From the legendary Bill Monroe to more contemporary heroes like Sam Bush and Chris Thile, and even including some non-bluegrass greats like Dave Apollon and Jethro Burns, this book contains a wide variety of music and playing styles to enjoy.

00195621............................................... $24.99

### THE MIGHTY MANDOLIN CHORD SONGBOOK

Lyrics, chord symbols, and mandolin chord diagrams for 100 pop and rock hits: Blowin' in the Wind • Crazy Little Thing Called Love • Dance with Me • Edelweiss • Georgia on My Mind • Hey Jude • I Feel the Earth Move • Jolene • Lean on Me • Me and Bobby McGee • Mean • No Woman No Cry • Patience • Ring of Fire • Sweet Caroline • This Land Is Your Land • Unchained Melody • Wonderwall • and many more.

00123221............................................... $17.99

### O BROTHER, WHERE ART THOU?

This collection contains both note-for-note transcribed mandolin solos, as well as mandolin arrangements of the melody lines for 11 songs: Angel Band • The Big Rock Candy Mountain • Down to the River to Pray • I Am a Man of Constant Sorrow • I Am Weary (Let Me Rest) • I'll Fly Away • In the Highways (I'll Be Somewhere Working for My Lord) • In the Jailhouse Now • Indian War Whoop • Keep on the Sunny Side • You Are My Sunshine.

00695762  Tab, Chords & Lyrics ...................... $15.99

### THE ULTIMATE MANDOLIN SONGBOOK

arr. Janet Davis

The Ultimate Mandolin Songbook contains multiple versions varying in difficulty of 26 of the most popular songs from bluegrass, jazz, ragtime, rock, pop, gospel, swing and other genres, in both standard notation and mandolin tab. Songs: Alabama Jubilee • Autumn Leaves • The Entertainer • Great Balls of Fire • How Great Thou Art • Limehouse Blues • Orange Blossom Special • Rawhide • Stardust • Tennessee Waltz • Yesterday • You Are My Sunshine • and more!

00699913  Book/Online Audio ........................ $34.99

# Great Method Books & Instruction for MANDOLIN

## Hal Leonard Mandolin Method
SECOND EDITION
*by Rich Del Grosso*

Noted mandolinist and teacher Rich Del Grosso has authored this excellent mandolin method that features great playable tunes in several styles (bluegrass, country, folk, blues) in standard music notation and tablature. The audio features play-along duets.

00699296 Book 1 Only .............................$9.99
00695102 Book 1/Online Audio ..............$16.99
00125223 Book 2 Only .............................$9.99
00125222 Book 2/Online Audio .............$14.99
00125547 Method Pack with Mandolin ...............................................$179.99

*Supplement Books also available:*
00695865 **Easy Songs for Mandolin**......................................$12.99
00695739 **Mandolin Chord Finder** (9" x 12") .........................$7.99
00695740 **Mandolin Chord Finder** (6" x 9") ...........................$5.99
00695779 **Mandolin Scale Finder** (9" x 12") .........................$7.99
00695782 **Mandolin Scale Finder** (6" x 9")............................$6.99

## First 15 Lessons: Mandolin
A BEGINNER'S GUIDE
*by Fred Sokolow*

The First 15 Lessons series provides a step-by-step lesson plan for the absolute beginner, complete with audio tracks, video lessons, and real songs! This mandolin book features video and print lessons on: mandolin fundamentals; music reading; tuning; chords; scales & basic theory; strumming; arpeggios; double stops; moveable chop chords; sawing & tremolo; and chord/melody playing.

00289021 Book/Online Media.................$16.99

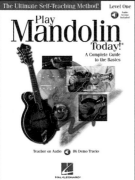

## Play Mandolin Today!
A COMPLETE GUIDE TO THE BASICS
*by Douglas Baldwin*

This mandolin method can be used by students who want to teach themselves, or by teachers for private or group instruction. Simply follow the tips and lessons in the book as you listen to the teacher on the audio. This complete guide to the basics covers: songs, chords and melodies; alternate picking and strumming; and playing tips and techniques, all in standard notation and tablature.

00699911 Book/Online Audio ...................$9.99
00701874 Book/CD/DVD Pack................................................$19.99
00320909 DVD Only .......................................................................$14.99

*Supplement Book also available:*
00115029 **Play Mandolin Today! Songbook** ...........................$12.99

 HAL•LEONARD®

Order these and more publications from your favorite music retailer at
**halleonard.com**

## Mandolin Blues
FROM MEMPHIS TO MAXWELL STREET
*by Rich Del Grosso*

Travel back in time as acclaimed mandolinist Rich DelGrosso traces the history and music of America's rich blues tradition through the eyes of the mandolinist. Follow the lives of players like Yank Rachell, Howard Armstrong and Charlie McCoy, and then learn their timeless music with standard notation, tab, and full-band audio of all the tunes in the book.

00695899 Book/Online Audio .................$19.99

## Fretboard Roadmaps: Mandolin
THE ESSENTIAL PATTERNS THAT ALL THE PROS KNOW AND USE
*by Bob Applebaum & Fred Sokolow*

This installment of our popular Fretboard Roadmaps series is a unique book/online audio pack for all mandolin players. The included audio features 48 demonstration tracks for the exercises that will teach players to: play all over the fretboard, in any key; increase their chord, scale and lick vocabulary; play chord-based licks, moveable major and blues scales, first-position major scales and double stops; and more! Includes easy-to-follow diagrams and instructions for all levels of players.

00695357 Book/Online Audio ................................................$14.99

## Hal Leonard Mandolin Fretboard Atlas
GET A BETTER GRIP ON NECK NAVIGATION
*by Joe Charupakorn*

Mastering the mandolin neck can be a challenge, even for very experienced players. The diagrams in this full-color book will help you quickly memorize scales and chords that may have previously seemed difficult to grasp. You'll be able to easily see and understand how scale and chord shapes are laid out and how they connect and overlap across the neck. The material is presented in all 12 keys, using complete 12-fret neck diagrams with color-coded displays of the most common fingerings.

00201829...............................................................$19.99

## 101 Mandolin Tips
STUFF ALL THE PROS KNOW AND USE
*by Fred Sokolow*

Ready to take your playing to the next level? Renowned fretted instrument performer and teacher Fred Sokolow presents valuable how-to insight that mandolin players of all styles and levels can benefit from. The text, photos, music, diagrams, and accompanying audio provide a terrific, easy-to-use resource for a variety of topics, including playing tips, practicing tips, accessories, mandolin history and lore, practical music theory, and much more!

00119493 Book/Online Audio ...............................................$14.99